Acting Scenes & Monologues For Kids!

Original Scenes and Monologues For Kids 6 to 12...Combined Into One Very Special Book!

by Bo Kane

"Acting Scenes & Monologues For Kids!"
Revised edition. April, 2014
First Printing December 2010
Burbank Publishing
212 S. Reese Pl.
Burbank, California 91506
Burbankpublishing@gmail.com

ISBN 0-9841950-1-7

Cover - Film Strip: Michael Grant, Austin Kane, Clinton Emmanuel, Megan Mercado, Avery Phillips, Hannah Mae, Lee Mekki, Will Babbitt, Karlin Walker, Makena Kane, Fionn James, Daniel Grzesiak, Paige Childs, Camilla Machado, Lela Brown, Victoria Grace. Group photo: page 101

Book Cover and masks designed by Thomas Cain

For Denise, Makena and Austin

My wife and kids have provided not only the inspiration for much of the material, but also the love and encouragement to get it done. I'm a lucky guy.

TABLE OF CONTENTS

Monologues:

TABLE OF CONTENTS

Acting Scenes

Who's Acting?

Every kid knows that acting is a great way to express yourself. And not just professionally: sometimes we act like a clown, act like we're innocent, act like a know-it-all. Sometimes we imitate/act like our parents (when they're not looking).

We also love to act like our favorite kids on tv or in movies, doing the scenes for our friends to make them laugh. Acting is fun. So, 'who's acting?' We all are!

And "Who's Acting?" is the answer to the age-old parent line:

> *"Stop acting like such a goofball!"*
> "Who's acting?"

Some of us may end up acting on stage or in television and movies. Some will act just for fun. Either way, being up in front of other people and playing a character, any character, is good training.

A guy named Shakespeare once said: *"All the world's a stage."* And he's right. Because whether you become a professional actor .... or a policeman, teacher, doctor, or store owner ..... **everybody** acts.

Foreword

This book is divided into two parts: acting by yourself (Monologues) and acting with someone else (Scenes).

During each monologue or scene a young actor will play a character, and that character will experience a change, a revelation, or will learn a valuable lesson. Sometimes the character is clever, sometimes serious, sometimes the character laughs out loud.

The themes are familiar: friendship, schoolwork, getting in trouble, getting or giving presents for a birthday, how to treat animals, and using your imagination.

Most of the monologues and some of the scenes can be played by either a boy or a girl with just a minor adjustment or two. A few, such as "Football For Real", should obviously be played by boys, and "Bully Girl" has two girls and one boy.

For Monologues, sometimes it's obvious who you're talking to; other times you may have to pick someone in your personal life. It's important to put yourself in your character's shoes. How do they feel?

Where are they? What happened just before you began to speak? What does your character want?

In the scenes where you will be working with another actor, it's very important to LISTEN to what the other character is saying. And to listen *as your character listens*: hearing it for the very first time.

It's also important to play the "pauses". A great actor acts when he has lines, and when he doesn't.

So your character is not only acting, but also re-acting to what the other character says. So, again (sorry to repeat myself, but this is kind of important) no matter how many times you heard the lines in rehearsal, your *character* is hearing them for the *first time*.

There's an old joke: *"How do I get to Carnegie Hall?" "Practice, kid, practice."* So, whether you want to be at Carnegie Hall, the stages of New York or the film sets in Hollywood: practice, kid, practice.

Let's do it. And have some fun.

Bo

MONOLOGUES

mon uh lawg - *noun*
a part of a drama, or comedic solo,
in which a single actor speaks alone;
soliloquy.

"Rich Without Money"

RORY

I wish my dad was rich. Morgan has a rich dad, and he travels all over the world. He brings her presents too, from everywhere. Big ones. I wish we were rich. Then I could have a swimming pool like they do, and a big new car. Morgan even has a nanny that takes care of her, and someone who cooks her dinner.

At our house, my mom cooks and takes care of us. And my dad comes home every day after work and plays with us in the back yard and shows us how to build things.

Morgan comes over here a lot, and we all play. I think she really likes it at our house.

I don't know why. It's not half as big as hers.

© Bo Kane

"Preventive Medicine"

ALEX, who has been invited to a class-mate's birthday party, sits in a chair with a worried expression. Finally gathers the courage to talk to Mom about the problem.

                    ALEX
Mom? Could you tell Tori's mom
that I'm going to be sick tomorrow?
That I have chickenpox or the
measles, or one of those dangerous
earaches or something? I …I don't
want to go to that party.
Those kids play so rough, they laugh
when you get hurt, and they spit their
food all over when they talk and …I
don't really like them that much.
    (gets an idea)
Hey! I know! Tell them I have the
flu, and with the money we save …on
the present that we don't have to
buy… we can go to the movies!

"All Things Animals"

A young News Reporter stands outside an animal shelter with a microphone.

REPORTER
Hi, this is Jo Baxter reporting for the "ALL THINGS ANIMALS" network. It's going to be a hot summer, so here are a couple of tips for your pets:

1)   Make sure your dogs and cats have plenty of water available all day long.
                 and

2)   NEVER leave your pet in the car in the parking lot, even if you crack the window.
The only "hot" dog that you want this summer …comes on a bun with mustard!

This is Jo Baxter reporting for "ALL THINGS ANIMALS".
Now back to you in the studio.

"What's Going On?"

DANNY runs in to the living room all excited….

                    DANNY
Wow! Were you guys watching that in here?! Iron Man just flew into this battleship and with one punch just annihilated that guy that had these electric whips ….
        (he stops. They're all quiet.)
What? What's going on? Why are you all staring at me?
        (He reads their faces)
Oh. Is this about the fire in the trash bin? Listen, I can explain that! We were just going to see if these papers would burn, but then it wouldn't go out. And when we closed the lid we thought it would suffocate 'cause they told us in school that fire needs air to breath. I didn't know it would melt the lid!
        *(he looks at their surprised
        faces)*
This is about the fire ….. isn't it?

Uh-oh. If Danny wasn't in trouble before, he is now.

Note from the Coach:

In the previous scene "What's Going On?" Danny
had a complete change of expression and emotion:
he began excited and happy, but quickly saw the
stares and had to backpedal.
Here's a girl's quick version:

DANIELLE excitedly runs into the room.

> ### DANIELLE
> Mom, mom! Did you just see that
> commercial!?! They have these new
> leopard-print tights that would really
> go with my dance top and ….
> *(sees their faces)*
> What? What's going on? Why are
> you all staring at me?
> Oh. Is this about the cat? It just kept
> coming around and I only fed it a
> couple of times! And it needed a place
> to sleep so I let it in the garage. I
> didn't know it would throw up in your
> new car. I tried to clean it up. *(pause)*
> This is about the cat, isn't it?

Danielle's mom motions her to come over
and sit down. She hangs her head and
walks (offstage).

"Story Problems Are Easy"

RILEY sits in the kitchen doing homework.
He (she) closes one book and opens another.

RILEY

That's it for spelling, now Math.
Story problems.   These are easy.
"If you're in a car going 20 miles per
hour and you drive for 15 minutes,
how far did you go?   20 miles an
hour!?!   What, is my ***grandmother***
driving?!   Six blocks.
(he writes, then reads)
If 12 make a dozen, what is a gross?
Mr. Kozinski's nose hairs.   That's the
<u>definition</u> of gross.   Next.   If plums
are 25 cents a pound, and you need 5
pounds, how much would you have to
pay?   HAVE to pay?!?   Zero.
(he writes)
I'm not paying anything for plums,
I hate plums.
This stuff is easy.

(S)He closes the book and walks away.

"Birthday TMI"

BAILEY

You know what we're doing today?
First we're going to the park, then
we're going to the movies, then we're
going to have pizza at Chuck E.
Cheese. And cake and ice cream.
You know why?
Because on this day, __7_ years ago,
at about 8:30 in the morning, my
mom leaned back in her hospital bed
    (she leans back)
and yelled
AAARRRGGHHHH!!!!!! …

    (sweet smile)
And there I was.
Today's my birthday.

"One Less Gamebuddy"

JAKE is in his room talking about his friend; (animated at first, then serious).

JAKE

My friend Wyatt lived just at the end of our block, and we used to do everything together. Walked to school, went to movies, had sleepovers when we were little. A few days ago I was playing my Gamebuddy, and I was doing better than I ever had. Wyatt knocked on the door and asked me to come over to his house, but I told him I couldn't 'cause this was my best game EVER. He told me it was important, and I told him "not as important as <u>finally</u> getting to Level 10!" He left, and I didn't see him for a few days. Then today I looked down the block and saw a big moving van in front of their house. I ran down there and the movers were just finishing. They said Wyatt moved out this morning. That's what he wanted to tell me. He wanted to say good-bye. But I was too busy playing my game.

Notes from the Coach:

* In "Rich Without Money", (pg. 11) why do you suppose that Morgan likes hanging out at Rory's house?

* In "Butter-Fly" (pg. 12), really see the butterfly (what color is it?), see it struggle, see it fly away. Take your time.

* Have fun with "All Things Animals". Use your own name if you like.

* In "Story Problems" (page 17) Riley is a character who really believes he/she has all the answers. Those answers make perfect sense to him/her.

* In "Birthday-Too Much Information" (page 18) Bailey's yell has to be real, as if you're in pain or lifting something heavy. A real (not phony-baloney) yell, followed by a nice sweet smile. Also, say your own age.

• In "One Less Gamebuddy" (page 19), try not to give away the ending as you tell the story. Show your enthusiasm for the game, though you know at the end it cost you a friend. In the end, be genuinely sorry.

"Tough Teacher"

DANA marches out of school, angry with her teacher.

DANA

When I grow up I'm going to be a teacher, and I'm gonna be ***nice*** to kids. I'm not gonna punish everybody just because one kid gets us in trouble ….. Carter.

Mrs. Johnson does that all the time, and it's not fair. So when I'm a teacher, everyone who was good will get to go home, and I'll be fair and just punish that one kid.

(gets more animated)

I'll make him stay after school by himself, and write a thousand times on the board, and I'll make him stand in the corner, and I'll ….

(pause; she realizes what she's doing)

I'll be just like Mrs. Johnson. Maybe I should just be a doctor.

"Pop Quiz"

JESSE walks toward his class and hears kids from the previous class talking about a quiz.

> JESSE
> A what? A quiz!? Oh no, today?
> I'm not ready for a … wait, it has to
> be on the Revolutionary War, that's
> what we've been studying.
> Washington, taxation without
> representation, Declaration of
> Independence. I got it. I know this
> stuff. I think. What if it's about the
> other one, the Civil War? No, she
> wouldn't.
> *(grabs his phone, checks the time)*
> One minute. Ok….what do I
> remember? ….Lincoln. Grant.
> Slavery. Gettysburg Address, 1860's.
> The Battle of the Monitor and the
> Merrimack …. Hey! I know this
> stuff, too. I'm there, A-City coming
> up. Bring on this test; Jesse Harrison
> … is in the house!

He strides into the classroom.

"I-phone, Me-phone"

WILL is in his bedroom complaining....

WILL
I can't stand the way my Mom
is always on her iPhone. No matter
where we go, she's not really there
with us, she's wherever the 'other'
person is. If I ask her something, it's
*"Can't you see that I'm on the
phone?"* I swear she likes that phone
more than she likes me.
(sits, thinks for a moment)
It is cool, though.   You can go to
these awesome websites, take
pictures. She let me use it one time,
and I took a picture of my sister then
gave her a long nose and mustache.
And then I was googling my dad's
favorite football team, and he called
right when I was doing it and I gave
him the score of his game!   How cool
is that?
But when I finally do get one of those
phones, I promise I'll look up from it
once in a while.   I'll own the phone.
It won't own me.

"Save The Drama For The Stage"

Megan talks about last night's rehearsal....

MEGAN

Ok. So we're supposed to be on stage at five, that's the only time we could get, and Rikki doesn't want to ride with Sarah, so Sarah's mom goes to pick up Lauren instead and Rikki decides to walk and she's late. And when they get there they all get into an argument and they want ME to side with Lauren who's mad at Sarah for something I don't even know about.

And Rikki suddenly doesn't feel like dancing so I'm trying to explain that nobody meant to hurt anybody's feelings and the next thing you know it's 5:30! The rehearsal is half over and we haven't even danced yet!

I got so sick of all the arguing, I hit the music really loud, and went up there and started our routine. I danced by myself for a while, then finally everybody stopped complaining and came up. And at the end of it, we had about a fifteen-minute rehearsal.

MEGAN (cont'd)

When I got home I called my big sister and told her what happened. She told me two things:

"*Stay out of it*" and "*Save the drama for the stage.*"

And that's what I'm gonna do.   Stay out of it.

(small smile)

I'd rather just dance.

Notes from the Coach:

*   "Pop Quiz" (pg. 22): Never heard of the Monitor and Merrimack? Hit the google button, Sparky; it's part of knowing your character. What does "A-City" mean? He just thinks he'll get an A; use your own expression if you like.

*   In "I-phone Me-phone" (page 23) Will doesn't have a complete change of heart: he's frustrated by the gadget, but he also realizes how cool it could be. Have fun with imitating Mom saying "Can't you see I'm on the phone?!" Do her voice.

•   In "Bad Words" (page 28), Lee gets two bad consequences – both the mom, and subsequently the dad, are mad at him. Play that line "*now we're both grounded*" realizing that his excuse got his dad in trouble too.
Take your time.

"Don't play the result. If you have a character who's going to end up in a certain place, don't play that until you get there. Play each scene and each beat as it comes. And that's what you do in life. You don't play the result."

- Michael J. Fox

"Science Camp"

ROBIN runs in through the door with a back-pack and a smile.

ROBIN

You wouldn't believe what I got to do at Science Camp this week! I got to shoot off a rocket, and we had real lab coats and goggles, and …. me and my science partner made a real robot! It was so cool! We made him out of real steel, and we hooked up the batteries and it worked! Then we raced all of the robots and ours won! First place! It was awesome.
You know what else we made? Slime! Real slime from real chemicals!
We learned so much stuff… did you know the sun is a star? We saw all the constellations. Maybe I'll ask for a lab coat for my birthday.
I think I'm going to be a scientist when I grow up.

© Bo Kane

"Bad Words"

LEE wears a sad look, explaining to a friend
why he/she isn't going to "Fun Zone".

LEE

I can't go. I got in trouble today. For
saying a bad word. It just slipped out!
My dad says it every time somebody
cuts him off in traffic, but **I** get
grounded for it.
And now my mom says I can't go to
Fun Zone.
So I said "if I can't go to Fun Zone
for saying bad words, why does Dad
get to go play golf on Sunday?! He
says 'em all the time!"
Now we're both grounded.
And all I said was ….

*(about to say the bad word,
looks around, thinks better of
it)*

I better not. I'm in enough trouble.

"Homework Ogre"

Shane is in the classroom explaining what happened to his homework....

SHANE

I did the homework, ok, but when I came out of my room with the papers in my hand, suddenly I could feel this big wind swirling in front of me. I took one more step, and I was sucked right into the vortex, and the next thing I knew, I was falling into a pit about a mile long! When I landed, there was this fire-breathing ogre who let out a fireball and burnt everything around me. I ran to get away, and when I was going toward this castle I found this sword stuck in a stone. I pulled it out and flung it at him and when it hit him he morphed into a giant bird, like in Avatar, and he swooped me up and carried me back into the vortex. It took all night to make the journey back, and when I got here... my homework papers were gone.

But I really did the assignment. I guess it just got burnt by the fire.
(lame smile)

29

"Tooth Fairy"

Cassidy is pointing to a tooth in the back of her mouth.

CASSIDY

I have a tooth coming out. It's this one, right down here.

(she points to a tooth)

I can wiggle it with my tongue. I'm supposed to wait until it comes out by itself, but I'm helping it a little bit. Because when the tooth comes out and you put it under your pillow, the Tooth Fairy comes. And you get money. She buys up all the kid's teeth, then takes them to a volcano and melts them. And then she makes piano keys out of them.

That's why when you see people playing the piano, they're usually smiling ---- the real teeth are smiling at their cousins, the teeth in the piano. It's true. My uncle told me.

30

"GOOAAALLL!"

ELIAS has a troubled expression on his face, and a baseball cap nearby. He loves his dad, and doesn't want to disappoint him, but he'd rather play soccer than baseball.

ELIAS

My dad wants me to try out for baseball. He was a great baseball player, but ... I ...
> *(his expression says "I don't really like it." Then, he brightens up...)*

I like soccer. Running down the sideline in the World Cup, get the pass and *(he kicks)* BOOM!
> *(He throws his arms up in the air like he just scored a goal).*

Gooooooaaalll!
> *(He takes in the crowd cheering for him, then. . back to reality).*

But my dad wants me to try out for baseball. So, I'm gonna try.
> *(puts his baseball cap on)*

Wish me luck.

He grabs his glove and heads for the door.

Notes From The Coach:

* In "Homework Ogre" (page 29) even though it's a big, unbelievable story, Shane is trying to convince the teacher ... so describe it vividly and (in Shane's mind) believably. If you see the bird, the castle, the vortex (whirling air, like a tornado) we'll see it too.

* In "Tooth Fairy" (page 30) in the middle of Cassidy's story, she makes a confession that she's "helping it a little bit". This would be a good place to try a **stage-whisper**, a loud 'whisper' that can still be heard far away.

* Elias (page 31) is very animated in the middle of "Gooaaallll!!!"--- he puts himself right in the middle of the soccer match. Be physical, kick your leg, and love that game. Maybe don't overplay the dread of the baseball game, just that you're doing it to please your father (which you really want to do).

* In "Girl Trouble" (page 34) does Jack really like Sarah?

* In "Two-Dollar Fortune" (page 35) Blake can show us his environment: does he or she have to whisper so Mom won't hear? Are there other customers waiting? Do we think the Clerk is smiling, or thinking "*No way, kid.*"? You can play it either way.

"Target Practice"

JAMIE sees Mom looking at herself in the mirror, combing her hair over and over. This is the perfect time ….

JAMIE

Mom. Hate to tell ya, but …your hair isn't looking so good. And I think I know the problem. Split ends. But you know what? They have a shampoo for that. At Target. Come on, let's go!
We'll take care of that little problem of yours right now.
(grabs mom's keys)
And as long as we're gonna be at Target, we might as well glance at those new video iPods. They even have one for 3-D. We should look at them while we're there. No sense making two trips. Let's go! I'll get your keys.

Jamie walks away from the bathroom smiling like (s)he's just pulled off the greatest trick in the world.

"Girl Trouble"

A Young Boy is trying to explain how he got into trouble at school.

JACK

It wasn't my fault. Sarah is always messing with me in class, especially when our teacher isn't looking. I think she likes me. But today she took my good pencil and wanted me to get it back from her, 'cause … I think she likes me.
So I chased her – just to get my pencil back – and when she went around the table she fell. It must have looked like I pushed her, but I didn't! Our teacher got mad and just wanted somebody to blame. And I didn't want to tell on Sarah about the pencil … I don't know why I didn't ……
and I didn't want the whole class to get blamed, so, …
I got in trouble.
        (*pause*)
Now I <u>know</u> she likes me.

"Two Dollar Fortune"

BLAKE walks up to the counter at a department store, looks over his/her shoulder to make sure Mom is not watching, then asks the clerk ….

> BLAKE
>
> "Excuse me; I have to buy something for my Mom. It's her birthday tomorrow. Can you help me? She likes soft things, like pillows, and scarves, and ... she's right over there…
> *(points)*
> … she likes boots, and she's really pretty so she likes to smell nice. And red. She likes stuff that's red.
> *(reaches into pocket and pulls out two bills)*
> I only have two dollars. Do you have anything I can get for her? I'm kind of in a hurry."

He/she looks at the clerk and offers the crumpled bills, really hoping, trusting, that she can help out.

"Snake"

CHARLIE, a boy with a lot on his mind, approaches his dad with a request.

> CHARLIE
>
> Dad? Can I get a snake? For a pet. It doesn't have to be a big one. Maybe just a little one, but still scary-looking. Like a corn snake or something.
>
> *(looks at Dad's questioning eyes)*
>
> See, some of the kids at school are mean to me … they don't think I'm tough. Because I'm not. But if I had a snake they'd at least think I'm kind of cool. And I only have to take it to school one time. That's all.
> I'll take care of it, I promise.
> Can I get one?

He looks up at Dad with pleading eyes. He really needs to up his cool.

"Mr. Pickles"

SOPHIA is sitting at a picnic table with two dolls, Mr. Pickles and Oscar, and some crackers and cheese.

SOPHIA

Mr. Pickles is hungry today, aren't you? Would you like some crackers and cheese?
(Mr. Pickles voice)
Why yes, I would like some crackers and cheese.
(Oscar voice)
Hey, what about me? I like crackers and cheese too!
(Sophia glares at them)
Aren't you forgetting something?
(Mr. Pickles and Oscar voice)
Oh, sorry. May we <u>please</u> have some? Thank you.
(Sophia voice)
That's better. Here you go. We have manners in our house. ….
All done? Ok, I'll eat the rest.
(sits back, eats, smiles)
I always get the leftovers.

INT. SPARSE BEDROOM   NIGHT

Turn of the century   A small bedroom with rickety furniture, and a young girl banished to it.   She pulls a doll out of her dresser.

                    SADIE
Well, Raggedy, it's just you and me agin. Gonna be here all night, no dinner.   I ain't hungry anyway, I had some bread on the way home from the schoolhouse.   And all that hollerin' and puttin' me in here don't upset me this time.   This time I got conviction. I know Pa thinks he's doin' what's right. But it ain't. There was a whole war fought over that, and that war is done but he's still fightin' it. Prob'ly be fightin' it 'til he's dead. That don't make it right neither. Either. Don't make it right 'either'. Miss Gwen would make me go to the board and do that sentence over again, wouldn't she?   Miss Gwen had us read the Declaration of Independence once. Right there in ink it said that all men are created equal.   Over a hundred

SADIE (cont'd)

years ago.   They might have been
created that way, but they sure don't
get treated that way.   So I get sent to
my room without supper for sayin'
hello to a colored boy. I don't care. I
got everything I need right here
anyway.   I got a window so I can
look out and dream, and I got
someone to talk to. Don't need
nuthin' else. Anything else. Sorry
Miss Gwen. I know you're helpin'
educate me.   In a whole lot of things.

"You Should Have Seen It"

JUSTIN runs into the living room and tells his (often-absent) dad about his great game. His dad barely looks up from his iPhone…

> JUSTIN
> You should've seen our game today!
> I was coming down the right side,
> Brandon kicked the ball on kind of a
> curve, like Beckham used to kick it,
> and I ran right up to the ball and
> WHAM!
> Slammed it right into the goal.
> *(makes a kick motion)*
> It was great!   Greatest day I've ever
> had. The whole team jumped on me!
> It was the only goal of the game!   I
> wish you could've been there, Dad.

His dad doesn't look up.   Justin sighs.

> JUSTIN (cont'd)
> You might have been proud.

Justin turns and walks away.

"Payback"

Zoe is on her cell phone at the mall.

                    ZOE
You wouldn't believe what I found, Sabrina!
The cutest lip gloss in Triple Shine Pink!
(listens) I'm at the mall. You are too! LOL!
I'll find you!
          (her phone buzzes, she looks)
Hold on. It's my brother.*(clicks phone)*
What, Philip? *(listens)* No! I can't hang
out here a few more hours until your
'girlfriend' leaves. I have dance class at six.
I need you to pick me up. You promised.
(listens) No, I can't just go to the movies.
You stole half my money!
          (listens, then mischievous grin)
Hey, Philip, you know who I just ran into?
Lauren! Your old girlfriend was right here
at the mall! I told her you were home and
that she should drop by and see you. Won't
that be nice? *(listens to You WHAT"!?!")*
Oh, that's right, you're with Amber. My
bad. Well, the three of you …
have a good time.
          (clicks him off, Sabrina on)
That'll teach him to keep his word.
Sabrina? Meet you at the food court.

She wears a sly grin as she walks to the food court,
then ….
                    ZOE
Hey, 'Brina? Do you have any money?

She walks off.

Notes From The Coach:

- In "Mr. Pickles" (pg. 37) Sophia does three voices: her own, and the two dolls. She could do one higher and one lower, or make up character voices. It might also help to put her hand behind the doll and move it as it talks

- In "Back In Time" (pg 38) Sadie has a particular dialect (way of speaking) and accent. Experiment with the language.

* In "You Should Have Seen It" (page 40) Justin doesn't know, until the very end, that his dad doesn't care. So he describes it with all of his enthusiasm and energy … until the end. As you play Justin, see the top of dad's head, maybe even see him raise his index finger, as if to say "One minute". But he never looks up. Justin still thinks he has a chance to make his Dad proud of him … until the very end. Then, he not only sighs, but his shoulders slump, his eyes turn sad … his whole body reacts. Maybe he could get a little mad at dad (?)

- *In "Payback" (page 41), Zoe takes the time to listen to Sabrina and her brother, and reacts to him telling her to, for example, "go see a movie" --and she says he stole half her money -- and hear him go crazy when she tells him she just sent another girl over to see him … and his new girlfriend. Have fun being devious.

Acting Scenes

Scene [seen] - *noun*
a unit of action or a **segment of a
story** in a play, motion picture, or
television show.

"I Before E"

MORGAN and ALEX are looking at their spelling homework.

MORGAN
Spelling doesn't make any sense! "Way" like "no way" is spelled right, but if I 'weigh' myself it's spelled w-e-i-g-h. G-H!?!

ALEX
It's weird, but it's right. "I before E except after C, or when sounded like 'A' as in neighbor and weigh."

Morgan glares at Alex.

MORGAN
You made up a rhyme for this?

ALEX
Somebody did. Weird, huh?

MORGAN
Ok, riddle me this, Batman. If the "gh" in weigh sounds like nothing, why does it sound like 'F' in 'enough'?

ALEX

I don't know. Why do they use a
"ph" to make the "F" sound in
telephone?

MORGAN

That's what I'm talking about! At
least in math, 2+4 always equals 6.
Not sometimes, all the time! In
spelling, 'gh' can sound like F, but so
can 'ph', and hey! Sometimes an
F sound is spelled with... an F!
Who invented this stuff?!

ALEX

Well, it's called "English" so take a
guess.

MORGAN

That figures. Anybody else would
spell "tea" t-e-e.
(English accent)
"What say, my lord; why not throw an
'A' in there just to mix it up a bit?"

ALEX

Ok, ok. You made your point. You
want to study math?

MORGAN

No.

ALEX

Ok then. Let's keep going. Spell 'knock'. Here's a hint: the first "k" is silent.

MORGAN

This is hopeless.

Morgan drops face-down in her book. She quits.

ALEX

Wait 'til we get to "imagination". The "t-i" sounds like an "s-h".

Morgan lifts her face just long enough to give an evil stare at Alex, then, drops it back down.

46

Notes from the Coach:

* In each scene it's very important to listen to your scene partner, hearing the dialogue as your character does: for the very first time.

* Your entire body is your instrument, not just your voice. Your voice will change with your emotions, and so will your facial expressions and body language. Don't be a stiff; let every fiber of your body match your emotion.

* An actor needs to be .... believable.

* Even if you paint your character with big, broad strokes, be believable. Nickelodeon and Disney casts play very big, sometimes cartoony characters, but because they stay **true** to their characters, we buy it.

* If you or your scene partner says the wrong cue or drops a line, it's no big deal. Stay in character and keep going. In real life, we don't always know what the other person is going to say.

"Football For Real"

AUSTIN and TREVOR are left in the living
room while their mothers go to the kitchen.

AUSTIN
So, what do you want to do?

TREVOR
Let's play something.

Trevor starts looking through his video toys.

AUSTIN
Let's play football!

TREVOR
We can't. I broke that game.

AUSTIN
I mean outside.   With a football.

TREVOR
Outside? Football for real?

AUSTIN
Yeah. I brought one. We can throw it
around in the front yard.

TREVOR

I've never really thrown a football
for real. But I can make Andrew
Luck throw it great on my game.

AUSTIN

Ok. You be him on the Colts. I'll
be Russell Wilson. Let's go.

He heads toward the front door. Trevor puts
down his video games, hesitates.

AUSTIN (cont'd)

And when we've worked up a
sweat, we'll come in and play
video games. Ok?

TREVOR

We're gonna work up a sweat?!

AUSTIN

Yeah. Come on!

Austin tosses the ball to Trevor, who
bobbles it like a hot potato. He follows
Austin out the door with a sigh and a
worried expression.

"It's Gonna Explode!"

A science kit with jars of colored liquid sits in front of ARCHIE. KASEY picks up a jar of blue liquid.

> KASEY
> Ooh, a chemistry set. Do you know what you're doing?

Archie takes the jar from him and swirls it.

> ARCHIE
> Of course not. That's why it's called an experiment. Let's pour that chemical into this one, and then mix 'em together.

> KASEY
> Cool. We can be like mad scientists.

Archie does a low, evil laugh as he holds his jar still. Kasey pours in the other chemical. They set it on the table, and watch.

> KASEY (cont'd)
> Oooh, it's smokin'!

Archie picks up another bottle.

ARCHIE
This says "never mix with
formaldehyde."

Mischief in their eyes...

KASEY
Let's do it!

They pour and watch the two liquids smoke.
Then bubble.   They laugh.

ARCHIE
It looks like it's gonna explode.

KASEY
Yeah. It might blow up.

Then, their smiles turn to *UH-OH!"*
Their eyes get big … then …...!!!!

ARCHIE
I'm outta here!!

KASEY
Wait for me!!!

They run out.

© Bo Kane

51

"Stolen Keys"

Taylor is in the library when Callie RUNS IN.

> **CALLIE**
> Here!   Hide these room keys!
> Whatever you do, don't tell Mrs.
> Baker where you got
> 'em cause I DIDN'T DO IT!

She drops them like a hot potato.

> **TAYLOR**
> Neither did I!...Do what?! Why do
> you have her keys?

> **CALLIE**
> Some guys were playing a trick on her
> and locked her out of her room, and
> they just shoved them at me and ran!

> **TAYLOR**
> So you just hand them to me?!
> Thanks a lot.
> (looks, thinks)
> I know.   We'll just leave them at the
> librarian's desk, then pretend we're
> sick and go to the nurse's office.
> When she finds them, we'll be way
> over there.

CALLIE

Great idea.   You're the best friend I
ever had.

They do a pinkie handshake.

TAYLOR

Friends forever.

They cough and sneeze their way toward the
desk, but just as they are about to drop the
keys and run...

MRS. BAKER (O.S.)

Girls! Are those my room keys?!?

They freeze in their tracks, eyes big.   Then-
--they turn and POINT AT EACH OTHER.

BOTH

She did it!!

(Mrs. Baker is an off-screen or off-stage voice).

© Bo Kane

"Tattle-Tale"

An older BROTHER sneaks into the kitchen, sees the candy jar. He looks around, then slowly lifts the lid. As he reaches into the jar and slooowly extracts a piece, he is STARTLED by …

LITTLE SISTER

Busted!!

BROTHER

Ahhh!!

The lid drops and makes a loud noise as he tries to catch it and fumbles it, making even more noise.

LITTLE SISTER
You're in trouble now.

BROTHER
You little … you better not tell Mom.

LITTLE SISTER
What'll you give me if I don't?

BROTHER
(threateningly)
You mean, what'll I <u>do</u> to you if you do.

She steps right up to him, not intimidated.

LITTLE SISTER

Then you'll be in even more trouble.

He knows she's right.

BROTHER

Ok, I didn't mean that. I'll be nice
to you for a week, just be quiet.

LITTLE SISTER

Two weeks. And a dollar.

BROTHER

A dollar! It's only a piece of candy.
(he thinks, gets a new strategy)
You know what? Go ahead and tattle.
Go ahead. Just remember: Nobody
likes a tattle-tale. Not even Mom.

He walks.

LITTLE SISTER

Ok! One week. And a quarter!

BROTHER
(over his shoulder)
Tattle-tale brat.

He's gone.

LITTLE SISTER
(to herself)
I've got to work on my negotiation skills.

Notes From The Coach:

* "I Before E" (pg. 44) is a fairly long scene (but, seriously, haven't you wondered about this spelling stuff before?). Anyway, if you need to, cut it down. Maybe cut from "Who invented this stuff?" all the way to "Ok, ok, just spell 'knock'. (p.s. did you get the joke behind "weird, huh?" "Weird" doesn't follow any of the rules!)

* In "It's Gonna Explode!" (pg. 50) you can just use a little bit of water …. and a little bit of imagination.

* In "Stolen Keys" remember that they are in a library, so adjust your speaking voices. Using props, like keys (dropping them like they're hot) can be fun; same with the quick change from 'best friends' to 'she did it!' Be expressive.

* In "Tattle-Tale" (pg. 54) both Brother and Sister have a change of strategy in mid-scene, so the actors will change their voice and body posture too.

"Skateboard Champ"

A REPORTER holds a microphone and interviews the new skateboard champ, CASEY FLASH.

REPORTER
(to camera)
Hi I'm Dana Smith, reporting from the Long Beach Skate Park where Casey Flash has just won the half-pipe championship.
(to Casey)
Congratulations Casey.

CASEY
Thanks Dana. The rest of these skaters are really good, but I guess I got lucky today.

REPORTER
It was more than luck. You really put on a show out there. What do you think won it for you today?

CASEY
I think the judges liked the 3-60 that I pulled at the end.   I got a lot of air, and had fun with the twist.
So, yeah, I think it was my ending.

REPORTER

And that 3-60 ending got Casey
Flash a first place trophy. Anything
you want to say to the skateboarders?

CASEY

Yeah. Have fun, catch some air, but
… (*points to his helmet*)
protect your brains. Wear a helmet.

REPORTER

Good advice, Casey.
(*wrap-up to camera*)
That's it from the Long Beach Skate
Park. I'm Dana Smith, now back to
you in the studio.

© Bo Kane

"Bugs"

CODY and KATIE are lying on the picnic
table looking at bugs.

CODY

Hey look at this one.

KATIE

What is it?

CODY

I think it's a June bug.

KATIE

Aren't June bugs brown?   This is
black.

CODY

Well, it's not a beetle and it's not a
rolly-polly. I know what those look
like.

KATIE

Don't squish it! It might be a daddy
bug going home to his wife and kids.

CODY

I'm not going to squish it.   I'm just
looking at it. Off you go, little bug.

He puts it into the grass.

KATIE
He's probably going to go home and say "Whew! You wouldn't believe what happened to me today!   I was almost flattened by a monster!"

CODY
(bug voice)
"But it wasn't a monster, it was 'Bug Hero Man!'"

KATIE
"And his super-powered friend, "Super Insect Girl!" Wait, that doesn't sound so good.   "Bug Hero Woman!"

CODY
C'mon, Hero Woman; let's see if we can find some more.

KATIE
Here's a rolly-polly. Don't be afraid little buggie, I won't hurt you.

They both gently touch the bug in her hand.

"I'll Cover For You"

AIDAN is cowering in the closet when his older sister MARLEY approaches.

> MARLEY
> Are you hiding from Mom?
> *(he nods 'yes')*
> How come?

> AIDAN
> I broke her favorite clock.

> MARLEY
> On purpose?

> AIDAN
> No! I was just swinging my light saber and I didn't see it.

> MARLEY
> Just tell her it was an accident.

> AIDAN
> But she's gonna be mad! She loved that clock. Grandma gave it to her.

> MARLEY
> Well you shouldn't have been swinging a light saber in the living room.

AIDAN

I'm sorry!

He begins to break down.   Marley feels for him, puts her hand out to help him up.

MARLEY

I know. Listen, I'll tell her I did it. I haven't been in trouble in a long time. Come on.

He takes her hand and gets up.   They turn, and look up to see MOM.

MARLEY
(to Mom)
Mom, I'm sorry, I didn't mean to…

AIDAN
(interrupting)
Mom I broke the clock and I'm really sorry. I promise to never do it again.
(to Marley)
Thanks anyway.

Marley puts her arm on his shoulder. He's growing up.

"Bully Girl"

A SMALLER GIRL walks up to a table with a lunch bag. Just as she pulls out a chair, a BIGGER GIRL grabs the chair and pulls it away like a bully.

SMALLER GIRL
Hey! I was going to sit there.

BIGGER GIRL
Well, now you're not.

SMALLER GIRL
That's not fair. You can't do that.

BIGGER GIRL
(in her face)
What are you going to do about it?

Unseen by the Bigger Girl, the Smaller Girl's big BROTHER walks up behind the Bigger Girl and towers over her.

SMALLER GIRL
I'll tell my brother. Or maybe I don't have to.

BIGGER GIRL
And why not, Squirt?

SMALLER GIRL
'Cause he's standing right behind you.

The Bigger Girl turns to see the BROTHER glaring down at her.

BROTHER
Don't ever threaten my sister. Got it?

The Bully looks up at him, then turns and runs out. The Smaller Girl sits down.

SMALLER GIRL
Thanks.

BROTHER
No problem. Hey, she doesn't have a big brother, does she?

SMALLER GIRL
She's got a brother, but he's only 4.

BROTHER
I can probably handle him.

SMALLER GIRL
Yeah. .... Probably. *(giggles)*

He thumps the back of her head as he exits.

© Bo Kane

65

"The Eyes Have It"

WILL and CLINTON are shooting squirt-guns at a target at the County Fair. Will is hitting well; Clinton is getting frustrated.

BOTH
Pow! Pow! Swoosh! Bam! Awww. Gotcha! C'mon! Awww.

They stop, out of time and quarters. Will gets a prize thrown to him.

WILL
Alright! That's the best I've ever done!

CLINTON
I hardly hit any. Maybe this gun is off.

WILL
I used it last time, and I won a prize then, too.

CLINTON
Yeah. And I didn't hit with that other gun either.

WILL
Maybe you need glasses.

CLINTON

Glasses!? I don't want to look like a nerd!

Will is about to be a wise-guy, and say something like *"too late, you already look like a nerd*!" But he stops himself from saying it when he sees how upset Clinton is.

WILL

Uh…you won't look like a nerd. You'll look smart. That's all.

CLINTON

You think?

WILL

Sure. Real smart. Smart is cool. C'mon. Let's go to the Funhouse.

They walk away, Clinton considering glasses, Will wears a *"whew, I almost insulted my friend*" look on his face.

© Bo Kane

"Music On The Fly"

CARLIN is reading when MAKENA enters.

MAKENA

Hey, are you going to be in the Talent
Show?

CARLIN

Actually …. no.

MAKENA

It'll be fun. I'm going to be in it.

CARLIN

Good for you. You're not doing that
retro Hannah Montana again, are you?

MAKENA

No! …I'm doing retro Miley. I'm
using her music but writing my own
words. Hey, you're really good at…

CARLIN

No.

MAKENA

I haven't even asked you yet.

CARLIN

No.

Makena ignores the 'no' and gears up to perform her song, to the tune of Miley Cyrus' *"Fly On The Wall"*

> MAKENA
> Here's the start: it's like Miley's
> "Fly On The Wall".....
> *(singing the chorus)*
> "Don't you wish that you could ace
> three tests in a row?
> Paint artwork that's so great
> It's in a gallery show."
> Lyrics about school.   Cool, huh?

> CARLIN
> (looks away, talk/sings)
> "Don't I wish that you would
> go away for a while.
> Being in a talent show is
> not my style..."

> MAKENA
> You got it! I knew you could help.

> CARLIN
> I could, but I'm not.

> MAKENA
> You can't or you won't.

CARLIN

I'm not.

MAKENA

I can't tell if you're chicken, or just
not as good as you think. I'll go with
chicken......buck buck ba-buck buck.

Carlin sighs. He puts his book down.

CARLIN

Do something about the teachers.
They'll all be sitting right there.

MAKENA

Like ...what?

CARLIN

Like .....(*talk-sing*)
"Don't you wish Miss Dunn would
give a test that's fair?
Ask questions that we studied
Not from 'who knows where?'"
You know, stuff like that.

MAKENA

I knew you'd say 'yes'. I'm signing
us up.

She runs out, excited. Carlin protests …

CARLIN
I didn't say yes, I ….

… to thin air. He's frustrated with himself.
As he picks up his book and walks out....

CARLIN (cont'd)
(to himself, to Miley's tune)
"Can't you just ... learn to keep
your big mouth shut?"

He smacks himself in the head with the
book.

"Pants on Fire"

Two kids are sitting at the school computer. ELLIOTT grabs the wireless mouse from SABRINA.

ELLIOTT
C'mon, let me play with it! Uh-oh.

It drops, shatters. He puts it into her hand.

ELLIOTT (cont'd)
Here, take this!

SABRINA
Don't give it to me! What are we gonna do? She's gonna find out and know we broke it!

ELLIOTT
So, we tell her we didn't.

SABRINA
What?!

ELLIOTT
We tell her we were just coming from the restroom and we found it like that. She's been in the front of the room, she won't know. We'll tell her we weren't even here.

SABRINA

That's called 'lying'.

ELLIOTT

Yeah, and your point is …?
Look, just do it right and we won't
get in trouble.

SABRINA

I can't lie!

ELLIOTT

'Brina, we're not …lying. Exactly.
We're acting. You always wanted to
be an actress. Just let me do the
talking, and you '*act*' like I'm telling
the truth.

SABRINA

No. I'm going to go tell her it was an
accident, and that my dad will get the
school a new mouse and that we're
sorry. That's the truth.

She gets up and walks to the front of the
room. He watches her go.

ELLIOTT

She's gotta learn how to act.

"Español"

EMILY sits practicing her Spanish when
MICHAEL walks up.

> EMILY
> *(to herself)*
> ¿Que paso?

> MICHAEL
> What are you doing?

> EMILY
> Trying to learn Spanish.

> MICHAEL
> Why?

> EMILY
> There's a woman who lives on my
> street, and she doesn't speak English
> very well. But she's really nice and
> makes cookies, so I wanna talk to her.

> MICHAEL
> That's cool. But everybody knows
> the word "hi". It's hola. You could
> just say that. Or just smile at her.

EMILY

I do, but I wanna do more than that.
Do you want one of her cookies?

MICHAEL

Sí, gracias. Hey, these are good!

She realizes he's speaking Spanish.

EMILY

That's right! Your mom speaks
Spanish. Say "these are good."

MICHAEL

Estos son deliciósos. Or just say
¡Que rico! One more?

EMILY

Ok. How do you say 'one more'?

MICHAEL

Uno màs. Maybe I should just walk
over there with you.

EMILY

Great! You should taste her fajitas.

MICHAEL

Whoa, this just keeps getting better.

And off they go.

"The Tryout"

JAKE and SARAH walk out of the school and down the sidewalk. Jake looks worried.

SARAH
You ok? What'cha thinking?

JAKE
My dad is making me try out for baseball. On Saturday.

SARAH
That's great. My dad loves baseball too.

JAKE
Well I don't. I'm no good at it. I'm gonna get killed out there.

SARAH
No you're not. I'll bet you're good at baseball. Have you been to the batting cage?

JAKE
No, that's just it. My dad hasn't had any time to help me; he just wants me to be great at it because he was good. But he's in New York until Friday.

SARAH

Want me to ask my dad to take us?
He loves to hit in the batting cage.

JAKE

You've been to the batting cage?

SARAH

Lots of times.   I'll bet my dad would
love to have a boy with us. Let's go
tonight. He'll help you hit. And
afterwards we go for ice cream.

JAKE

Ok.

Jake is stunned with gratitude.

SARAH

I'll call you when my dad gets home.

JAKE

Thanks.

She waves, walks away. Jake's face changes
from afraid to anticipation. He pretends he's
facing a pitcher, and hits a pretend double.

77

Notes from the Coach:

*   Our "Skateboard Champ" (page 58) is a
humble champ. He's proud of himself, but
he's no braggart. (If you want to make him
a braggart, just adjust a few lines and give
him some attitude).
For our Reporter, it's best to hold the mic in
the hand nearest the Champ, and tilt it back
and forth for the lines.

*   In "Bugs" (page 60) you can use prop bugs,
or your imagination.

*   In "I'll Cover For You" (page 62) Aidan is
near tears because he knew he shouldn't
have been playing like that in the living
room. He knows that it's his mom's gift that
she loves, and he might be punished. He
grows up in this scene, and is willing to take
his punishment.

*   In "Bully Girl" (page 64) we'll need to see
some real affection from the brother and
sister at the end of the scene, as she's teasing
him and he thumps her (gently).

*   Will has to make a quick facial expression
change in the middle of "The Eyes Have It"
(page 66). He **almost** teases his friend, but
decides (in an instant) to **be** a good friend
instead. Both he and Clinton should have
fun shooting at the beginning, but soon
Clinton realizes that he's not hitting
anything. Have fun making your own
sound effects.

Notes from the Coach:

*   For "Music On The Fly" (page 68) you may
    have to check iTunes or YouTube if you
    don't know the tune. Carlin is making these
    lyrics up as he goes; saying them for the
    very first time. He's good at it, but he
    shouldn't make them up too fast.

*   In "Pants On Fire" (page 72) Elliott sees
    nothing wrong with lying to get out of
    trouble. In his mind, it's perfectly ok.

*   In "Español" (page 74) Michael doesn't
    have to be Hispanic, but he should speak the
    Spanish convincingly. In his mind, all that
    good food is a good trade for a few Spanish
    phrases.

*   In "The Tryout" (page 76) Jake goes from
    worried to hopeful … with a little help from
    his friend. Let his gratitude show. And at
    the end, when he takes a few pretend swings
    before he leaves -- be animated! Hit a
    pretend homer!

"Smackdown"

A BROTHER is watching TV when his
SISTER enters.   Seeing her, he quickly
changes the channel to Discovery Channel.

SISTER
What are you watching?

BROTHER
Uh,… this. …. Whatever it is.

SISTER
What WERE you watching?
   (she grabs the remote, hits
      'back')
Fighting?!

BROTHER
It's Friday Night Smackdown!
Boom! Choke-hold! The Master of
Disaster!   Aaarrrghhh!

He punches the air, then fake flexes.

SISTER
Does Mom know you're watching
this!?

BROTHER
No, don't! …..she doesn't need …

She yells out as she leaves the room.

                    SISTER (cont'd)
          MOM!   Did you know Blake is
          watching people beat each other up!?

She's gone. He plops back down, hits the
remote back to the Discovery Channel.

                    BROTHER
                  (to himself)
          She does now.

"Take It From Me, Kid"

Louie is starting his first day at school, and his big brother Isaac is giving him the inside story.

ISAAC

Now that you're going to real school, you need to learn a few things about teachers and classrooms and stuff.

LOUIE

Like what?

ISAAC

Like, in kindergarten they let you just throw your backpack on the floor. Not anymore, buddy. You get a locker.

LOUIE

Really? Cool!

ISAAC

Yeah, and you don't go home at lunch time, either. You eat lunch here. And here's a tip: always use a straw. 'Cause if you tip your milk over your mouth some kid will bump you, trust me. And you'll be wearing your milk.

LOUIE

I can still take my Power Rangers to
the lunch room, can't I?

ISAAC

Uh, sorry, Louie; no Power Rangers.
You're all grown up now.   Gotta
leave 'em at home.

LOUIE

I…I..can't?

Louie looks shocked, almost ready to cry.

ISAAC

Ok, you know what? Take 'em in
your backpack. And if your teacher
finds 'em, tell her your big brother
said it was ok. I've still got a lot of
pull around here.

Louie shoves them into his pack, smiles a
'thanks'. Isaac puts his arm on his shoulder.

ISAAC (cont'd)

I think you're ready, kid. Let's go.

"Cousins"

Two kids ride the bus home from school.

MARSHALL
Hey, Zoe, what are you doing this
weekend?

ZOE
On Saturday I'm going over to my
cousins'. They live on a ranch and
they just got a new dog that's
gigantic!

MARSHALL
Wow, cool. I wish I had cousins.

ZOE
You don't have cousins? Everybody
has cousins.

ZEKE
Not me. My mom is an only child
and my dad's brother hasn't got
married yet.

ZOE
That's too bad. Cousins are like your
friends, but they're your family too.
It's like a double friend.

MARSHALL
I know. I just don't have any.

Zoe thinks about it for a moment.

ZOE
I'll be your cousin.   We'll tell people
that our moms are cousins. That
would make us like …. second
cousins or something.

MARSHALL
Yeah! Like cousins once replaced.

ZOE
Yeah.   And maybe you can come and
see the dog with me. You want to?

MARSHALL
I'll ask.

The bus pulls to a stop, Zoe gets up.

ZOE
Me too.   See you later, cuz.

Marshall smiles. She has a cousin.

"Sleepover"

SABRINA and CAITLIN are walking down
the school hall…

CAITLIN

I've got to go home and practice
piano so I can go to Amber's slumber
party. It will be so cool. I'll see you
there.

SABRINA

Uhh … I don't think so.

CAITLIN

What? You were invited.

SABRINA

Yeah, I was invited last time, too.

Sabrina gives her a *"remember?"* look.

CAITLIN

Oh, yeah, the water trick. Sorry. But
you know that we were just having
fun….and we know you have a great
sense of humor.

SABRINA

Yeah, right.
                (more)

SABRINA (cont'd)
Look, I have dance, homework, and music lessons … and I go to bed early. And I NEVER want to be the first one to fall asleep at a slumber party. Never again.

CAITLIN
You won't be! And even if you did, we won't play any tricks on you. I promise we won't.

SABRINA
Thanks, but … have fun.

CAITLIN
What?   Don't you trust us?

They look at each other for a long moment.

SABRINA *(softly)*
No. It was really embarrassing, so … no. See you Monday.

Sabrina walks away. Caitlin starts to call after her *("okay, fine!")* but doesn't. She stands alone in the hall, figuring out that you can't just ask for trust. It has to be earned.

© Bo Kane

87

"Unnecessary Roughness"

JAKE catches up to COBY after school.

> JAKE
> Hey, Coby! Try-outs for flag football are tomorrow. Did you forget to sign up?

> COBY
> No.

> JAKE
> I didn't see your name on the list. Did you ask your mom?

> COBY
> Yeah.

> JAKE
> What did she say?

> COBY
> Did you see my name on the list?

> JAKE
> No.

> COBY
> That's what she said.

JAKE

Oh, no, you gotta play football.
Who's gonna throw the ball to me?

COBY

Don't know.

JAKE

Why can't you play?

COBY

My mom says it's dangerous and she
doesn't want me to get hurt.

JAKE

Does she know that you don't tackle
in flag?   That nobody gets hurt?

COBY

I don't know.

JAKE

You didn't tell her that?!   You gotta
tell her.   She probably thinks we
tackle.

COBY

Yeah, maybe.   I didn't think of that.

JAKE

Come on, we need you at quarterback.
I'll go home with you and we'll tell
her together.

COBY

You will?

JAKE

Sure. I need somebody who can pass
the ball to me. Let's go.

Coby follows him with a new hope and a
new sense of purpose.

Notes from the Coach:

*   In "Sleepover" (page 86) does Sabrina really want to have this conversation? She might be a bit uncomfortable with it, or is she still mad about the trick? Two choices. Same with Caitlin: she could be a nice girl who's offended by the lack of trust, or she could be a not-so-nice girl who wants Sabrina to fall asleep so she could play another trick on her.

*   In "Unnecessary Roughness" (page 88) Coby starts out sad/frustrated, but ends up with a ray of hope. Jake needs him (Coby is the only decent quarterback) so he's going to try anything---even talking to Coby's mom. Play him with some energy.

*   There are shocks that are bad (spill your milk all over your homework) and shocks that are good (reach into your pocket and find a lost 5-dollar bill). In "Trading Lunches" (page 92) Jordan gets a bad shock (he just traded away his favorite lunch) and Darby gets a good shock. Be expressive. Don't let your expression give away what's in the lunches until you open them.
And yes, "Lunch-munchie" can be hard to say; it's a good time to practice enunciation (speaking clearly).

*   In "I'll Say A Word..." (page 94) Lindsey likes being in control, but in the end learns a lesson, and the regret shows on her face.

"Trading Lunches"

Two kids sit down in the school cafeteria. JORDAN looks at his lunch box, looks over at DARBY's, and without even opening his to see what in it, JORDAN offers to trade.

                    JORDAN
          Wanna trade lunches?

                    DARBY
          Maybe.   What have you got?

                    JORDAN
          I don't know.   It's a surprise.

                    DARBY
          Like a peanut butter and jelly
          surprise?   I don't think so....

                    JORDAN
          I'll throw in 50 cents.

                    DARBY
          Hmmm....ok.

He takes Jordan's lunch, opens it up and --- a really good shock.

                    DARBY (cont'd)
          Whoa! Lunch-munchies! Alright!

JORDAN
Lunch-munchies?!? Mom didn't tell
me she bought me Lunch-munchies!

DARBY
I love these!
(*starts eating*)

JORDAN
Me too.
(*He opens the other lunch.*)
And your mom made peanut butter
and jelly. Great.
You know, there's enough in that
Lunch-munchie for both of us.
(Darby ignores him)
At least give me the 50 cents back.

Darby thinks about it, then slides only one
of the quarters over.   Jordan looks at his
sandwich, and half of his money; sighs. He
made a bad trade.

JORDAN
I stink at gambling.

"I'll Say A Word…"

LINDSEY and ALLISON are trying to do
their homework, but just aren't into it…

> LINDSEY
> Hey, let's play a game. A word game.

> ALLISON
> I really need to get this done…

> LINDSEY
> Come on! Here's the game: I'll say
> something, and you say the first word
> that comes to your mind.

> ALLISON
> How do I know if I got it right?

> LINDSEY
> There's no right or wrong, you just
> play.

> ALLISON
> Ok.

> LINDSEY
> Ok. Uh … "cat".

> ALLISON
> Ping pong.

LINDSEY
What? That doesn't make any sense.

ALLISON
You said there wasn't any right or
wrong.

LINDSEY
There's no right or wrong, but there's
'weird'. And that was weird.

ALLISON
You make up the rules and then get
bossy with me when I don't play the
way you want? Go play by yourself; I
have homework to do.

She buries her face in her book. A pause.

LINDSEY
Ok, you don't have to get mad. It's
just a game. I said I was sorry.

ALLISON
No, you didn't. And by the way, my
cat sleeps on the ping-pong table

She nods/waves 'good-bye', not looking up.
Lindsay's face drops as she leaves.

"Try"

JACKIE is drawing on a piece of heavy
paper when TAYLOR walks up.

TAYLOR
What'cha doing?

JACKIE
Making my mother a Mother's Day
card.

TAYLOR
You're <u>making</u> it? Wow. Did you
draw this?

JACKIE
Yeah. Now I'll write a little rhyme or
something. You should try it.

TAYLOR
No, I'm not really good at drawing.
Or rhyming. Or …anything.

JACKIE
Yes you are.

TAYLOR
No, it's true. I'm kind-of good at a
lot of things, but I'm not <u>really</u> good
at … anything.

She holds up the pen, offering it to him.

                    JACKIE
    Try.

                    TAYLOR
    No, I can't. I'll just buy her a card…

                    JACKIE
    Try.   Stop making excuses and… try.

                    TAYLOR
    I don't know…

                    JACKIE
    And you'll never know. If you don't
    try. Ok?

                    TAYLOR
    Ok. I'll try.

She leaves. He picks up the pen and paper,
and, muttering to himself ….

                    TAYLOR (cont'd)
    'Thank you Mom, for all you do'.
    I love it when you make a stew….

'Hey, I'm kinda good at this. Who knew?'

"Famous"

TRACY glides in singing while HILARY
sits paging through a dictionary...

TRACY

(singing)
Sen-sational! Famous and sen-
sational. I'm gonna be hotter than
hot! Like it or not! Sen-sational!

HILARY

Hey. Hot stuff. Can you sing "Far,
far away"?

TRACY

I'm not sure I .... oh, I get it. You're
clever. When I'm a star will you
write stuff like that for me? Because I
AM going to be famous.

HILARY

Good for you.

TRACY

Oh, don't be jealous. We'll still be
friends when I have thousands of
adoring fans. I'll be on tv, in
magazines, photographers will be
taking my picture everywhere...

"Famous" (2)

HILARY

Yeah, think about that. People will
always be running after you, cameras
always clicking, and … they might
take bad pictures of you on purpose.
Happens all the time.

Tracy considers the horror of a bad picture
of her in a magazine. Then, …

TRACY

Nah. Besides, I can have my agent
photo-shop them for me.
Think of it, Hilary—you can write
songs for a famous singer.

HILARY

Yeah. And when you walk down the
street and all the people rush past me
to mob you, the only one who'll be
running to me, is you. I'll have the
songs, you'll have all the autograph
hounds.

TRACY

Won't it be great!?!
(dancing away, singing)
I'm going to be a shining star. Super
hot, brightest star in the galaxy….

Tracy dances away. Hilary pages through her dictionary.

> ### HILARY
> Hmm. Star: noun. A ball of gas held together by its own gravity.

She shakes her head 'yes' in agreement. Nothing needs to be said. She closes the book, looks off to where Tracy has gone, smiles to herself and walks away.

"Whether he's playing big and broad, or small and understated, an actor has to be ... believable."

- Bo Kane

Acknowledgements

This book would not be possible without the kindness of the folks who run On Your Mark Studios – Brian and Cinda Scott, Sam Hixon and Grady Beard.

Also, my wife Denise Loveday-Kane was not only patient and encouraging through the entire process, she read and advised me on every scene and monologue.

Tom Cain designed the book cover, and served as a sounding board and inspiration all along the way.

A thank-you to Makena and Austin Kane, and my brothers Ted and Dick Kane, whose life experiences became scene material. Another thank-you to John McCarthy, casting director extraordinaire, and Erica Babbitt .

And a huge thanks to all of my acting students, past and present, who come in to class every week with enthusiasm, talent, and a willingness to help the old coach with these scenes and monologues. Some of them are pictured on the cover and on the opposite page.

Bo Kane's On-Camera Acting Class

Back row: Fionn James, Langston Keyes, Daniel Grzesiak, Nathan Grzesiak, Makena Marie Kane, Karlin Walker, Michael Fahey. *Middle*: Mads Finegan-Smith, William Tao, Will Babbitt, Austin Kane. *First row*: Camilla Machado, Megan Mercado, Hannah Mae Burnworth, Shelby King.

About The Author

As an actor, Bo Kane has worked in television shows such as Criminal Minds, Castle, CSI: Miami, Dexter, 90210, Workaholics, Outlaw, FlashForward, Men Of A Certain Age, The Unit, and films such as The Ringer, Camouflage, and Man Of The House. He began his career in the 80's, appearing in such films as El Norte, Child's Play, The Phantom, What's Love Got To Do With It (as Dick Clark) and in television shows such as JAG, Melrose Place, The X-Files, Arli$$, General Hospital, The Magnificent Seven, and many others.

As a writer, Bo is a former newspaper columnist, penning "Man's Eye View" for the Sun-Times News Group, and "Hollywood Hoosiers" for The Times. He and Denise are the authors of *"The Wild World of The Wilder Kids"*, a tv movie in development.

Bo has worked on farms, in steel mills, as a newscaster for CBS affiliates, and for the U.S. Congress. He was the Head Coach for the Special Olympic Equestrian Team in the San Fernando Valley for many years, and is a graduate of the University of Notre Dame.

Aside from his acting and writing career, Bo currently teaches kids' acting classes in Los Angeles. He also coaches his own two kids in baseball and basketball, causing him to use way too many sports metaphors in acting class.

"I love working with kids. Their eyes are bright, their laughs are genuine, and their world has endless possibility."

- Bo Kane

Also by Bo Kane -

"Acting Scenes... and Some Monologues... For Young Teens"

ages 13 to 16